SELF-PUBLISHING CHILDREN'S AND YA BOOKS

ALLI'S GUIDE TO KIDLIT PUBLISHING FOR AUTHORS

ALLIANCE OF INDEPENDENT AUTHORS

CONTRIBUTOR: KAREN INGLIS

SELF-PUBLISHING CHILDREN'S AND YA BOOKS
ALLi's Guide to Kidlit Publishing for Authors

© 2024 Orna A. Ross, Second Edition.
First edition 2021.
Alliance of Independent Authors

EBOOK: 978-1-917292-00-9
PAPERBACK: 978-1-917292-01-6
LARGE PRINT: 978-1-917292-02-3

The authors' moral rights have been asserted. All rights reserved.
Enquiries: info@ornaross.com

✽ Created with Vellum

CONTENTS

Preface by Karen Inglis, author of The Secret Lake (A UK & USA bestseller) — v

PART I
UNDERSTANDING THE CHILDREN'S BOOK INDUSTRY

1. Publishing for children — 3
2. Self-publishing a children's or YA book — 9
3. Popular genres for children and young people — 15

PART II
STEPS TO PUBLICATION

4. Self and professional editing — 21
5. Interiors, illustrations and covers — 31
6. Printing and Distribution — 37
7. Building your brand and community — 43
8. Meeting young readers — 49
9. Marketing a children's book online — 55
10. One book, many formats — 63

PART III
RESOURCES AND SUPPORT

11. Frequently Asked Questions — 69
12. Resources — 71

Acknowledgments — 75
Other Guides — 77
About ALLi — 79

PREFACE BY KAREN INGLIS, AUTHOR OF THE SECRET LAKE (A UK & USA BESTSELLER)
ALLI'S CHILDREN'S PUBLISHING ADVISOR

If you'd asked my 10-year-old self what I wanted to be when I grew up, it certainly wouldn't have been a children's author. Up until age 14, I spent every spare moment helping out at the local stables, earning my rewards in free rides–and later with the pony I finally convinced my parents I deserved. (My older sister, meanwhile, was devouring *The Borrowers*, Enid Blyton and all the rest back at home.)

As I grew older, I dropped the ponies, and my mind turned to boyfriends, bilingual secretarial work, and living my life out in France. Alas, this didn't happen—but I did get the French degree and spent a year living in Tours.

My first job was teaching English as a foreign language where I quickly fell into writing the weekly lessons for a rolling syllabus. My later roles all involved writing one way or another, culminating in over 30 years as a professional copywriter, consulting to government, and the financial sector. It was during this time I had the idea for my first children's story.

As I suspect might be the case for many reading here, this was when my children were toddlers, and I spent hours reading to them—adoring some books, but loving others far less, and wondering if I really

Preface by Karen Inglis, author of The Secret Lake (A UK & USA bestseller)

shouldn't try my hand at this. (Household favorites *Hairy Maclary from Donaldson's Dairy* et al, and *Six-Dinner Sid* are still up in the loft.)

Like so many other writers, I went through the process of sending my stories out to agents and publishers only to receive back (in those days) the brown envelope with the single-paragraph rejection. It was disheartening (not least when I had a close shave with Bloomsbury) to the extent that I finally packed all of my writing, including *The Secret Lake*, into a box and went back to my day job for 10 more years. Fast-forward to December 2010 and a year's sabbatical, and I discovered the term "self-publishing" when searching (this time online) for agents.

From that moment, I didn't look back.

With my professional writing background, I knew I had to do it "properly"—and that was hard. I was all at sea on my own back then—getting to know print gurus in the online forums of Amazon's early self-publishing platform, CreateSpace; spending literally days trying to format a Word file ready for print; then giving up and outsourcing to my newfound formatting friend, Doug, over in Texas. I later spent a full week trying to format the same file for Kindle, this new e-reader thing that was suddenly all the rage. No one ever said it would be easy—but it really was the Wild West.

For those of you just starting out, or thinking about self-publishing, I promise those days have long gone. The writing and planning and rewriting don't get any easier, but there are great support groups, podcasts and courses to help with this, as I'm sure you know. However, compared with just a few years ago, we now have at our disposal a plethora of tools and online platforms that make self-publishing so simple compared with the early days. By this I mean technically simple. This is especially true when it comes to formatting your books for publication, finding specialist freelancers to help you complete your project, and tools to help you create collateral marketing material to promote your book.

We also have wonderfully supportive organizations such as The Alliance of Independent Authors (ALLi), whose thriving member group is both a safe haven and a place to get advice if you are stuck or need moral support. The organization is now working closely with the Society

Preface by Karen Inglis, author of The Secret Lake (A UK & USA bestseller)

of Children's Book Writers and Illustrators (SCBWI) to support its children's book authors.

Last, but by no means least, the marketing opportunities that have opened up to authors in the last few years have been game-changing for me and many other children's authors I know. Until this happened, 95 percent of my sales had been face-to-face at school or book signing events. I achieved close to 10,000 sales by the end of 2017 that way—and that was no small feat—but without a marketing team behind me, it was hard to scale up.

Love them or hate them, Amazon and other online retailers now enable us to reach our buyers. Parents, grandparents, aunts, uncles and siblings—and anyone else who is shopping online for children's books—can now see our books as they browse the site. From the moment indie authors were given space on this online table alongside traditionally published books, things started to change. And this is an opportunity for everyone. As I write this in 2024, *The Secret Lake* has now sold more than 500,000 copies.

If you have a children's story that you can't find a home for that has been written from the heart and put through all of the required stages of research, drafting, writing, rewriting, feedback and review as well as professional editing and proofing, there is no reason you can't self-publish that book and get it into the hands of hundreds if not thousands of readers, without breaking the bank.

All of which is to say, welcome to ALLi's guide to self-publishing books for children and young adults. I was honored to be asked to contribute to it, and I have shared, at appropriate points and at a high level, much of what I have learned over the last 10 years of self-publishing.

Karen

PART I
UNDERSTANDING THE CHILDREN'S BOOK INDUSTRY

Books for young people are a distinct arena of publishing with particular demands and challenges. This guide draws on the expertise of ALLi members and particularly ALLi's Children's Publishing Advisor and international bestselling indie author Karen Inglis.

1

PUBLISHING FOR CHILDREN

For children and young adults, books are not just pages bound together; they are windows to new worlds, mirrors reflecting their own experiences and doors to endless possibilities.

A successful children's book pleases two readers: the child who enjoys the reading and the adult who purchases the book. While adults are the ones who make the transaction, the children are the ones who will decide whether the book will be enjoyed or even treasured. You must keep the children in mind as you write and the adults in mind as you publish.

First comes the writing. Beware of writing about children as some adults might see them: as cute and comical sub human-beings. What children actually want is stories where they are the heroes, driving the action, facing the challenges, and making choices that lead to good outcomes.

Ask yourself:

- Why do I want to tell this story?
- What is my story about?
- Is this idea and theme going to be relatable to children?
- Is it unique?

- Is it marketable? What would make it more marketable (and pleasing to more readers)?

Recall what you liked to read when you were that age. Bounce ideas off children you know. Consider suggestions, explore and experiment, wander down different creative avenues.

RESEARCHING THE MARKET

Knowing who your readers are and what they want is key to successfully self-publishing a children's or young adult (YA) book. You need to know what makes them tick—what catches their eye, how their attention span works, what inspires laughter or curiosity.

Hang out with young people of the same age as those you want to write for. Read to them and tell them stories to see their imaginations in action. And hang out with your own inner child. What fills you with joy and a sense of adventure?

Read at least 100 children's or YA books, for research and inspiration. Take yourself off to the kids' or YA section at your local library or bookstore. Read the classics as well as lots of contemporary books, especially those that are winning awards.

As you read, you'll notice similar themes or character behaviors that make for good storytelling. If there are pictures, pay attention to the way they work with the text on each page. Make notes about anything that jumps out at you, appealing or unappealing, and how it might guide you to craft your own book.

Research the market for your kind of book, considering its ideal age-group, genre, niche and micro-niche. Children's literature ranges from baby board books to YA novels, so your target age range may be anywhere from 0 to 18. It's important to know your target audience's age range so you can deliver what your readers expect in terms of length, style, topic and treatment.

Understanding these things enables you also to keep those purchasing adults in mind, shaping your publishing choices so your book will actually sell.

Age Ranges

The age range of your book is the foundation of your publishing, from editing to designing to marketing. The closer you can keep to the market conventions of the particular niche of publishing that you're in, the more readers your book is likely to reach and the better it will sell.

The age ranges below are indicators and guidelines accepted by the industry, but should not be viewed as restrictive. Obviously, reading ages vary a lot between individual children. So use these categories as a general guide to think about the right category of reader for your book.

Books for all ages, and in all genres, should capture the young readers' imagination and inspire them to put themselves in the story. The reading experience—whether fiction, non-fiction or poetry—should be fun, with engaging and exciting outlines, a strong narrative voice, and a new and original angle on the perennial topics that challenge young people.

Picture books (ages 0-6)

A picture book relies on both illustrations and words to tell the story, and the wordcount is low, usually under 500 words. Board books for babies and toddlers can have fewer than 100 words, but still need a strong story and are far more challenging to write than you think—until you've tried.

Picture books are about character change, a moral or a lesson. A strong takeaway is expected, without belaboring the point. They must entertain the adult who will buy them as well as the child who will read them or have the book read to them. These are the books that inculcate a love of reading, right from the start.

Early readers (ages 6-7)

After picture books comes early reader fiction: books for children who enjoy books with more words than pictures, but aren't yet ready to tackle long blocks of text. These books can be read with adults and are designed to encourage a child's reading journey and nurture their emerging reading skills. Short accessible sentences and chapters, together with colorful characters and concepts, are needed to build confidence in new readers.

The "early reader" wordcount ranges from 2,000 to 5,000 words, though you'll still get your fair share of illustrations. Such books often come in a series, so kids can devour one after another.

Chapter books (ages 7-9)

From early readers, children progress to chapter books. Chapter books have a greater amount of text than picture books, and so the text has to be divided into chapters. The wordcount is higher, around 5,000 to 10,000 words per book. Although you'll still see pictures in chapter books, they are less important to the story than in a picture book and are often sketches rather than full-color illustrations.

Chapter books may contain elements of mystery. Many invite children to think about their emotions. Some prompt the reader to come up with solutions or even predict how each story will end.

Middle grade (ages 9-12)

Middle-grade books are typically 30,000 to 50,000 words, with even fewer illustrations, perhaps even no pictures at all, except to accompany chapter headings. This is when young readers start identifying which genres they like and dislike, choosing favored books and authors, and perhaps even introducing their parents and teachers to new books.

The book's main character is usually the same age or slightly older than the reader, and the subject matter features issues that pre-teens experience in their own lives—things like making friends, family issues or school dynamics.

YA (teens)

Teenagers are compelling creatures, caught between childhood and adulthood, with raging passions fighting growing responsibilities. This rich emotional backdrop means YA books often appeal to many readers who are older than the target group.

This category differs from other children's books in that YA readers buy books themselves, no longer completely relying on parents or teachers to choose for them. Perhaps that is why YA has emerged as a powerful literary genre in the 21st century, generating and leading important conversations about gender, sexuality, race and identity.

The above tips come from John Fox, who offers more tips on writing a children's book at TheJohnFox.com/how-to-write-a-childrens-book/

Themes

In addition to age group, children's books are also categorized by theme. To research where you fit, google "children's book" and a phrase that describes the book you have written or want to write. Once you've found books that are similar, study the book descriptions. Figure out how your book is different and distinct while fitting that description.

Are you writing in a trend that is growing in popularity? Take your research further by browsing through the books at your local bookstore, library or online on Amazon to see what new children's titles are being released, what kind of stories they tell, and what topics they cover. For instance, children's books showcasing diverse cultures are on the rise, as are those about famous historical figures.

This research into the industry should by no means dictate your work, but it does inform you about the tastes of children as well as the concerns of parents and educators who are currently buying books like yours. Keep them in mind along your publishing journey.

Perhaps you have a professional expertise, social mission or personal passion that would make a good book for the children's or YA market. There are several ALLi members who are doing this:

- Tracy Borgmeyer writes books on science, hoping to inspire girls to love the subject. She also keeps in mind the adults who will ultimately make the purchase, so she includes resources for teachers: Shelovesscience.com.
- Kinyel Friday writes books on self-growth including self-confidence, self-esteem and other aspects of development that children (and even adults) might struggle with: Kinyelfriday.bigcartel.com.
- Marci Cox is using her personal experience to support families through cancer and help children make sense of an illness: Florpublishing.com.
- Julie Day writes fiction books for various age groups featuring characters with autism: Julieaday.co.uk/books-for-children.
- Peta Rainford uses activities and books to encourage children to learn about and reduce plastic pollution: Dogpigeon.co.uk.

- Carolyn Armstrong writes earth-friendly fiction for children: Ckabooks.com.
- LMB is a group of three authors, Linda Bessellieu, Tawana Bessellieu and Jaliyah Bessellieu-Webb, who write stories about diversity and culture: Mybessprojects.com.
- Lynn McLaughlin writes fiction that helps children focus on their emotional well-being: Lynnmclaughlin.com.

2

SELF-PUBLISHING A CHILDREN'S OR YA BOOK

Those of us who read or were read to as children still recall those books with the sense of joy, adventure and wonder they inspired.

Writing and publishing for young people is a responsibility, a privilege and enormous creative fun. By fostering the love of the written word at a young age, children's book authors help to nurture and grow the next generation of readers.

The process of becoming a children's author is different for everyone —there are many tools available to you and many pathways you can take. It's important to clarify your creative intentions from the start.

YOUR CREATIVE INTENTIONS

Ask yourself what you want to achieve from self-publishing a children's book. Is the process more about personal creativity, or professional advancement, or a business? Will you just do this one book or do you want to build a career, or an authorpreneurial enterprise, that includes merchandise, video and audio as well as books?

If you are aiming to sell your book and earn from it, that will influence your content and design choices as well as your publishing, distribution and marketing approach.

Becoming a successful children's book author, earning a living from your books, is challenging. There's a lot of competition, not least because people with little experience think it's easy. But there is no harsher critic than a child, who will not hesitate to drop a book and say, "it's no good."

You must publish children's books because you love them, and not because you think they are a fast track to acclaim or money.

YOUR PROCESS

It all begins with writing the book! So many people talk about writing but they don't get on and do it. All authors—whether self-published or not—have to make a commitment to their writing, so create a routine that fits into your life, ideally writing every day, especially if you're new to creative writing or you haven't been writing for a while.

Alice Hemming, who writes across several age groups from picture books to teens, describes how she fits her author work alongside the responsibilities of being a parent.

"As soon as the children are out of the door, I head to my writing shed at the top of the garden and work on my longer work in progress. To keep me on track, I use the focus booster app to work in short, highly focused bursts, with the Pomodoro Method. I use WriteTrack.cloud to help me organize word targets for each day and to keep track of how I'm doing."

Alice also makes space in her day for the other necessary tasks of author life. "I try to meet my target in the morning, then in the afternoons I'm free to catch up on other writing projects, email, critiques, website and everything else. Of course other things always crop up, like (virtual) meetings, (virtual) school visits, and (actual) sick children, so the plan is flexible."

SELF-PUBLISHING

Self-publishing was once considered a last resort for authors unable to find a suitable publisher, but is now seen as a positive choice with many advantages. Crucially, it's a great way for children's book writers to keep control of their work, both creatively and financially.

You no longer have to depend on traditional gatekeepers to reach your readers. ALLi's Children's Publishing Advisor Karen Inglis has books for a range of reading ages. She says: "Self-publishing means we can get our stories out to our readers more quickly than waiting to be discovered by a publishing house."

You can publish books with themes that you have a personal connection with—as we've seen with the examples of ALLi members who spotted a need for books related to their interests in science and ecology, or their experiences with cancer or autism.

In short, you are the creative director not just of your books and their content, but also of your publishing business—because when you self-publish, you are in business.

As with any publishing project, self-publishing a children's book relies on both writing and publishing skills.

Karen says: "As well as writing the book I organize everything else—including finding an illustrator and cover designer, finding beta (test) readers, editors and proofreaders, getting the book interior designed and formatted (I do some of this myself, but not all), then uploading to the printer or Amazon. Once the book is up, there's all the marketing to do—so that people know it's available and can buy it."

To begin with, the multitude of tasks can seem overwhelming. For now, keep an open mind as you read the information ahead and know that ALLi is here to support you through your self-publishing challenges as they arise, which they certainly will. But also keep in mind that the ability to self-publish widely, and the great tools that enable self-publishing, mean there has never been a better time in publishing history to be an author.

Also know that thousands of indie authors have been where you are and have overcome the obstacles to self-publish successfully.

Advantages and challenges

There are multiple advantages and challenges in self-publishing, but many can be overcome by developing an indie mindset.

Indie authors relish the advantages of self-publishing, which are:

- You're not tied to the topics the publisher is interested in, for instance, writing to trend instead of the material you feel personally drawn to.
- You can have a direct conversation with your readers, and can better meet their needs.
- You can provide additional resources to your readers to create a comprehensive ecosystem around your books, which builds a long-term relationship with them and keeps them coming back to you.

The challenges are:

- You may meet resistance from schools, libraries, festivals, and other institutions and gatekeepers. However, this is becoming less common as more curators learn about self-published author success.
- Writing for young readers is a constant balancing act between fact and fiction as children are impressionable. And as there are no gatekeepers to vet the content, indie authors need to take on this responsibility.
- Children's and YA books are evolving all the time, particularly as more of them have access to technology at a younger age and attention spans reduce. With no publisher to guide them, indie authors have to keep abreast of these changes themselves.

Perhaps the biggest challenge of self-publishing is developing an indie author mindset. This emerges in different ways for different authors. To distort Shakespeare's *Twelfth Night*, some indie authors are born independent, some choose independence, and some have independence thrust upon them.

The born indies come into writing through self-publishing. For them, it's the obvious and only choice. Then there are those who consciously choose self-publishing for its creative and commercial rewards: the speed, the control, the direct relationship with the readers. And then there are those who come to it uncertainly, perhaps after trying other routes. With time and dedication, they can also do well.

FURTHER READING

You can learn more about developing and honing a creative approach to publishing in *Creative Self-Publishing: ALLi's Guide to Independent Publishing* by ALLi director Orna Ross. You can purchase a copy at Selfpublishingadvice.org/Creative or, as an ALLi member, you have free access in the members' zone. Just login and navigate to PUBLICATIONS.

Alice Hemming, Interview in *People of Publishing*. Peopleofpublishing.com/post/i-want-to-be-a-children-s-book-author

3

POPULAR GENRES FOR CHILDREN AND YOUNG PEOPLE

From the first picture book a child holds to the complex YA novels that resonate with teenagers, literature is a companion through all stages of development. Each genre in children's and YA literature serves a unique audience, with different interests, emotional needs and cognitive abilities.

In the earliest years, picture books, with their vivid illustrations and simple narratives, ignite the imagination of young children and introduce them to the simplest stories. Then they start to encounter genres like fantasy and sci-fi, and a wider variety of storytelling modes such as interactive books. All of these offer them an escape into other worlds, sparking creativity and a sense of wonder.

As they develop into young adults, they encounter more complex themes and diverse narratives. These books do more than entertain. They also challenge their thinking, encouraging critical analysis and a deeper understanding of societal issues.

In our rapidly changing world, all the genres of children's and YA literature are constantly evolving, embracing new themes and storytelling techniques and formats. These genres collectively contribute to the holistic development of young individuals, nurturing not just their intellect but also their emotional and moral development.

In short, children's and YA literature offer tools for life, equipping readers with the skills, knowledge, and empathy needed to navigate their journey through childhood and beyond.

FICTION

Contemporary fiction

Contemporary fiction is a great way to address important topics using story to reach the hearts and minds of young readers, as many ALLi members are, in the examples in Chapter 1 "Publishing for Children".

Historical fiction

Young readers particularly relish the difference between times past and present. Historical fiction is defined as a story set in a time frame 50 years or more before the story was written.

Mystery

Mystery is one of the most popular genres in children's literature. Young readers love solving the case, following the thread of the unknown, catching the bad guy, and uncovering the truth.

Fairy tales and fantasy

This genre encompasses fairy tales, fables and fantasy books. Fairy tales have been a classic tradition in children's books for countless generations —Cinderella, Snow White, Hansel and Gretel, Rumpelstiltskin, and The Three Billy Goats Gruff have a long legacy.

Fables have a long tradition too and are usually short stories with a clear moral lesson, such as Aesop's Fables.

Fantasy books are an extension of this. In fantasy, you'll find stories about universes that are very different from the real world—places that operate under magic rules, where the typical laws of nature don't apply. Fantasy stories take varying approaches to the realm of possibility. High fantasy takes place in a totally different world, while low fantasy novels keep things relatively real, while introducing fantastical elements. Some authors use fairy tales as a starting point and create new stories or new retellings of much-loved classics.

Science fiction (sci-fi)

If you love sci-fi, it's likely you know a child or a parent who does too. Sci-fi retains (some of) our world's laws of physics and often explores an environmental or existential problem from our current lives, while setting the story in the future, or on other planets or universes and using elements of advanced technologies.

Horror

Horror books act out our darkest fantasies and fears, though often in a fun way and children's horror stories usually have a resolution that restores the world to right. Even very young readers can enjoy horror, as we see at Halloween. Some horror books have lovable monsters and creepy crawlies.

Other realistic fiction

This might include any of the adult genres such as romance and adventure, suitably angled to relate to a young reader's world. It also includes books that are tied to an interest such as ballet, football or ponies.

NON-FICTION

Biography/autobiography

Both biographies and autobiographies can be written for young audiences to tell the true story of an inspiring person.

Educational

Books are the most educational object in most children's lives. Popular topics are history, geography and sciences. There are hundreds of enlightening books on these and other topics, so if you want your book to stand out, you need a unique angle—such as the Horrible Histories.

Self-help

Self-help books help young people deal with the challenges they are meeting in life, from starting a new school to losing a pet or a parent. These books aim to bolster young people psychologically and emotionally.

POETRY AND VERSE

This is a broad category that encompasses picture books with accompanying verses to poetry books and verse novels for YA readers.

Young people are particularly open to rhyme and rhythm and don't have any of the hangups that older people sometimes bring to poetry. They love all kinds of poems, from nonsense verse to narrative epics and a good poem can span different countries or cultures, lifetimes and experiences, histories and the seasons, in the space of a few lines.

Children, like adults, turn to poems when emotion is high. Poems, like all literature, teach young people about empathy and tolerance and give them a few, well-chosen words with which to meet various aspects of life.

The best poems for young people make them laugh or cry, while considering the world anew. They can even inspire some children to try penning a few lines of their own.

PART II
STEPS TO PUBLICATION

Now you understand the publishing market for children's and YA books, you need to get your own book ready. In this section, we discuss the publishing processes using examples from ALLi members.

4

SELF AND PROFESSIONAL EDITING

We strongly recommend you hire a professional editor. But before you do, you should polish your manuscript as much as possible.

There are several aspects to self-editing and they go well beyond cleaning up typos.

SELF-EDITING

Self-editing should be done in two stages:

1. Deepening and developing

This is the redrafting and rewriting you do when you have finished your first draft. The types of questions you should ask yourself include:

- Does my book have a clear story or structure that is engaging for my target readers?
- If it's fiction, are the characters memorable, with distinct voices?

- Is the language too complex or too simple for my target audience?
- If it's fiction, have I fully developed the turning points in the plot?
- Have I given the reader the history or back story necessary to make sense of the characters and action? Why do the characters do what they do?
- Am I avoiding any element or theme because it demands difficult emotional work or research?
- Is anything else missing?
- What is this book about?
- Does this fit into my original intention? If not, am I happy with the result or do I need to rework?
- What has changed since I started the book and should I adjust some of it with this new understanding?
- Does this do what I want it to do? What is that—entertain, amuse, inform, support, comfort, challenge? Perhaps several of these things?

The best question, the one that encompasses them all, is this: have I taken the reader on a journey to help them see more clearly?

2. Correction and clarification

Successful self-editing requires you to be analytical. You need to hover over your book looking at it as an entity, in all its constituent parts—chapters, scenes, paragraphs, sentences and words. As stated above, you need to ask yourself: what does the reader need from me here to see more clearly?

Many writers do this by finding ways to make the work look fresh. For instance, not editing on the computer they usually work on. A change of perspective can give you a better overview. Try printing off a copy of the book on wide margins with double spacing—so you have lots of room for making corrections and noting ideas as you go.

As you read, keep in mind what you're trying to effect with each new page. What point are you trying to establish, what sort of mood are you trying to create, what background or context are you trying to suggest?

It's also good to read aloud as you go—perhaps in front of somebody else or into a recording device so you can play it back. Children's books, especially for younger readers, are often read aloud. But even if your book is for older age groups, reading aloud is a valuable way to spot awkward phrasings, unnatural dialogue and pacing issues. Listen to the rhythm and flow of the language and also the bigger ideas.

Also keep an editing notebook by your side and make notes to self.

Other tips for effective self-editing

- Take a break first. Don't edit when you're still close to the work. Step away from the manuscript, then you'll have fresh eyes when you return.
- Keep your target age group in mind. Ensure the language, themes and complexity are appropriate for their understanding and interest levels. For very young children, use simple sentences and concepts; for older children, you can introduce more complexity.
- Check for clarity. If it's fiction, make sure your story is easy to follow.
- Check for plot holes and inconsistencies, for instance in character details or story settings. Children are very attentive and can be confused by inconsistencies.
- Engage the senses. Children's books are often rich in sensory details. Make sure your writing paints a vivid picture, engaging readers through sight, sound, touch, taste and smell.
- In fiction, ensure any characters are well developed and relatable. Readers should be able to see parts of themselves in the characters or learn from their journeys.
- Again, in fiction, check dialogue. Ensure any dialogue sounds natural and is appropriate for the age of your characters. Avoid making young characters speak in ways that are too mature for their age.

- Check for themes and morals. Many children's books have an underlying moral or theme. Ensure this message is clear but not preachy. It should be seamlessly integrated into the material.
- Check use of visual elements. If your book will include illustrations, consider how your words will work with them. If the illustrations are telling part of the story, leave space for them to do their work.
- Cut unnecessary words. Children's books are typically shorter than adult books, so every word must count. Remove any passages that don't contribute to the story or character development.
- Ensure grammar and spelling are correct. This is crucial not just for professionalism but also because children's books can be a tool for language learning.
- Repeat the process. Self-editing isn't a one-pass task. Go through your manuscript multiple times, focusing on different aspects each time (story structure, character development, language).
- Stay true to your voice. While it's important to keep your audience in mind, also ensure that your unique voice as an author isn't lost in the editing process.
- Do the removing first, then the moving and improving, so you don't waste writing hours doing small edits on a paragraph or page or chapter that is destined for the trashcan.
- Take it slowly. Editing is a meticulous, sometimes plodding, process. Give yourself lots of time. Work in bursts—say, 90 minutes—then take a break. Patience and attention to detail in this phase will significantly improve the quality of your book.

Seek feedback

Once you've done your editing, get feedback from others.

Now is the time to find beta readers. These are individuals who read a manuscript and provide feedback from the perspective of an average reader. Their role is crucial in the writing and publishing process, particularly for self-publishing authors. Beta readers might include children's librarians, nursery or primary school teachers, parents, and children in the target age group that (ideally) don't know you.

Your test audience should include both children and adults. They will each comment on different aspects. For instance, younger readers will tell you whether the book held their attention, and they'll give it to you straight. Adults can comment on more complex elements such as themes.

Also seek feedback both from other experts in children's book publishing. These might be fellow authors or editors who know the target audience well and can provide expert commentary and suggestions on the areas you considered in your self-edit.

You might also want to enter competitions for unpublished work. These can be an excellent way to get feedback. They also give you a deadline to work towards.

Take all the opportunities for feedback that come your way. You never know where they might lead.

PROFESSIONAL EDITING

Every writer needs at least one professional editor. We do not see our own work clearly, and an experienced set of eyes is essential to catch mistakes and oversights in our manuscripts, no matter how perfect we think they are.

A professional editor can do more than catch mistakes. They can help you strengthen your work in all ways. The editor Stephen Roxburgh helped Roald Dahl to extensively develop *The BFG*, *The Witches*, and *Matilda*. Together they tackled everything from major plot points to whether Dahl should describe confectionary as "candy" or "sweets".

In an interview with *Publishers Weekly*, Roxburgh recalls: "I ... discovered that with Roald all I had to do was ask good questions and leave it to him to come up with answers. It was a process he revelled in."

Dahl, in turn, felt so indebted to Roxburgh that he gave him his signed, dedicated, hand-bound proof of *The First Forty-Nine Stories* by Ernest Hemingway, with the author's annotations. It arrived with a note that read, "Dear Stephen, here is a tiny present—for all the help you've given me. Yours, Roald."

If this legendary and brilliant children's author benefited from the help of an editor, so will you.

Good editors are invaluable. In the early stages, they might add ideas, ask open questions and suggest solutions. More than that, they will appreciate and reinforce your creative intentions. This type of editing is called developmental – the editor helps you shape the content for your audience. In the later stages, once the content is working well, editors will help with the finer details such as logic, facts, consistency, spelling and grammar (copy editing) and final checks (proof-reading).

It's important to understand the differences between these types of editing – developmental, copy editing and proof-reading. They each take a different amount of time and require different input from you, the author. As you become more experienced, you may require less input at some of the stages—for instance, developmental editing. The various processes are also costed in different ways. For a detailed explanation, see *Creative Self-Publishing: ALLi's Guide to Independent Publishing* by ALLi director Orna Ross. This guidebook is free for members, and available to purchase for non-members at Selfpublishingadvice.org/Creative.

With children's books, editorial time and costs are likely to vary by the age group your book is aimed at. This of course affects the length of the text, complexity of plot, use of language, number and nature of any illustrations, and suitability of themes—all of which need evaluation.

WHAT TO LOOK FOR IN AN EDITOR

Genre and subject

No matter what you publish, you must select an editor who has substantial experience with your kind of books. For children's and YA books, you want someone who knows the age group you are writing for and the genre if appropriate—for instance, middle-grade fantasy or young readers picture book.

If your work is non-fiction or tackles emotional or sensitive themes, look for an editor with experience of this type of book. In some cases they may also recommend sensitivity readers.

Is an editor a good match for you?

How do you know if a prospective editor is a good fit for your work? For books with a longer word-count, such as middle-grade novels or chapter books, you might ask them to edit a short sample of your writing to determine if their comments are helpful and in tune with your aims and needs. But sometimes a sample won't tell you how an editor will handle your book in its entirety, particularly for developmental edits. You can also gauge whether you're compatible from a conversation, either voice to voice or by email.

In the case of picture books, sample editing isn't realistic. An editor might take a look at the book in its entirety and provide short commentary about the nature of required fixes along with a quote.

HOW DO I CHOOSE A TITLE?

Your title has to do a lot of work. It must grab the right readers and be memorable. Your editor will help, but here are some rules of thumb.

1. Use similar first letters (alliteration).

If your book is about Amy's adventure finding a meadow full of poppies, where she befriends a mouse:

- Don't call it *Amy's Adventure with Poppies*.
- Do call it *The Mouse in the Meadow*.

2. Don't use a descriptive title.

Many writers aim to describe the contents of their book in the title, but this can be dull. For instance, a story about a boy who is searching through a vast library to find a special book about eternal life.

- Don't call it *The Vast Library* (boring).
- Also don't call it *The Library Hunt*. (However, this is better.

"Hunt" is a good, active word, and the combination with "library" is intriguing.)
- Do call it *How to Live Forever*. (This is the actual title, and it's great. It's the name of the book the boy is searching for, it's interesting, and it lets the reader know deep topics will be discussed.)

3. Think about action and energy.

A lackluster title will spoil your book's chances for sure. Use fun, active verbs rather than passive ones.

- Don't call it *Johnny's Wonderful Day*.
- Do call it *Captain Johnny Defeats Dr Doom*. (Captain Johnny is more playful. "Defeats" is an active verb and "Dr Doom" uses alliteration.)

4. Use the technique of mystery.

Does your title provoke the reader's curiosity? Aim to give enough information that the child or parent will say "That sounds fun."

- Don't call it *The Bird in the Window*.
- Do call it *Oh, the Places You'll Go!* (What places?)
- Do call it *Olivia Saves the Circus*. (How? We want to know.)
- Do call it *How to Catch an Elephant*. (Tell me more!)

5. When you've identified a good title, google "Children's Book [Your Title]."

You want to see if it is already taken or if there is a title that is too similar. What if your perfect title is already used? Can you still use it? You can, because titles can't be copyrighted. But you'll have a hard time distinguishing your book from that book, so it's not always the best idea.

6. Test your title with your target audience

This includes adults if appropriate. It's important to see how readers react to your title. Are they excited? Do they seem bored?

FURTHER READING

Interview with Stephen Roxburgh. "Gobsmacked! Memories of editing The Witches." *Publishers Weekly* Publishersweekly.com/pw/by-topic/childrens/childrens-authors/article/58194-gobsmacked.html

ALLi has several titles that explain editing and other publishing processes. You can purchase copies of these guidebooks at Selfpublishingadvice.org/bookshop/ or, as an ALLi member, get free access in the members' zone. Just login and navigate to PUBLICATIONS.

5

INTERIORS, ILLUSTRATIONS AND COVERS

Illustrations, interior layout and book covers are vital aspects of any book, but particularly for younger audiences who are looking for a visual experience as much as a textual one. The look and feel of the book is entirely created by skilful use of colors, fonts and images, both inside and out.

INTERIOR LAYOUT

In the adult market, most indie authors publish first in ebook as that's where most of their sales are. But the majority of children's books for ages 0-12 are sold and read in print, so this is the most important format you'll make. However, there are good reasons to also create an ebook version. So once your print layout is finalized, you can make files that can be read on e-readers.

Your print book needs to be laid out and exported as a PDF, which will be sent to the printer. How do you do this? Assuming you're not a book designer, you have three main options. Much depends on the complexity of your book layout.

- DIY. This is feasible for books that are predominantly text, such as middle-grade novels and chapter books with a fairly simple design. The layout can be done in Word if you are competent using styles or other simple tools such as Vellum.
- DIY with ready-made children's book templates. A range of styles is available for picture books, illustrated chapter books and middle-grade novels that you can drop your content and any images into. These require some technical know-how, so it's worth researching whether you'll be comfortable using them.
- Outsource to professionals. This is recommended for picture books and also for middle-grade novels or illustrated chapter books if you are looking for quirky non-standard layouts. These can be worth the investment as they'll greatly add to the appeal of the book and help it stand out.

How easy is DIY?

This depends on your book type.

The older your reader, the simpler your task. Older readers are happier with books that are mostly text, and that makes layout much more straightforward.

In the case of middle-grade novels with no illustrations, you decide on the font, type size, line spacing, chapter heading and scene break designs, and front and back matter design. It's possible to do all of this in Word if you're competent with formatting, and convert it into the files needed for print and ebook production. Some of the sales platforms, for example Amazon's Kindle Direct Publishing (KDP), will provide you with free templates to create the book interior. Other frequently used design programs include InDesign and Affinity Publisher, but they require more expertise. As previously stated, another option, if you have access to a Mac, is a tool called Vellum.

For books with black and white illustrations, there is more to think about. You have to decide where to place the images to create a pleasing design. You'll also need to ensure the images are the correct quality for printing and that they are saved and inserted at the right resolution, otherwise they might be fuzzy, too dark or too faint when printed. If this is beyond your competence level, you might be better to outsource.

For picture books, DIY is not a recommended option. Even the simplest choice, such as a font, could make all the difference. A professional designer will save you a lot of time and trouble. They'll also know what is appropriate for your target reading age.

INTERIOR ILLUSTRATIONS

The success of a children's picture book depends on its illustrations. You absolutely need an experienced illustrator for this. They will understand how to enhance your written material, how to draw characters that will appeal to your target age group, how to compose the pages, important trends in styles, and technical considerations such as how the images will reproduce in print and how to convert them for an ebook version. Even if you're good at drawing, you might not have these other skills, so an experienced illustrator is a vital part of your team.

You can find an illustrator in the SCBWI illustrator gallery and the *ALLi Self-Publishing Services Directory*. This directory is free for members, and available to purchase for non-members at Selfpublishingadvice.org/directory.

Find out more about illustrations in ALLi's blog post "The Ultimate Guide to Illustrations in Books" at Selfpublishingadvice.org/the-ultimate-guide-to-illustrations-in-books/.

When to brief your interior illustrator

Although you might want to search for an illustrator early, don't send a detailed brief until you're sure the story won't change substantially. This usually means waiting until you're well into the copyediting stage and the overall structure is fixed and, for picture books, when your storyboard flows satisfactorily. You might want to create a rough mock-up with placeholder stick drawings, to check the flow.

How tightly should you brief your illustrator? Discuss with them how you'll work together. Some are happy to be briefed for each illustration. Others prefer to have the freedom to interpret for themselves.

The next stage is pencil drawings so that changes can be made if necessary. Once you're happy, the illustrator can produce the finished, colored and inked illustrations.

COVERS

Your cover is the first thing that readers will see, so it must package your book to attract your target audience. If the interior has a lot of illustrations, the cover will probably use an image from the interior or another image by the same artist so the look and feel is the same as the inside.

If you're hiring a cover designer, the principles are similar to those for hiring an illustrator. Look at the work of several designers to find one that chimes well with your book's content. Make sure they understand your target age group. Start your search early, because the good designers are usually booked several months in advance. Don't ask them to start work, though, until you're sure the text won't change substantially. Books can change a lot in developmental editing, especially novels. If you commission the cover too early, you might find it emphasizes themes and settings that you later changed.

When the designer starts work, you can expect the process to take a few weeks. Find out more about in *Creative Self-Publishing: ALLi's Guide to Independent Publishing* by ALLi director Orna Ross. This guidebook is free for members, and available to purchase for non-members at Selfpublishingadvice.org/Creative.

AI TOOLS FOR COVER ART AND INTERIOR ILLUSTRATIONS

AI tools are advancing all the time. Although it's a contentious area and there are pitfalls, plenty of authors are using them to create illustrations, as well as book cover elements and marketing images. ALLi has guidance on using AI Selfpublishingadvice.org/ai, which is regularly updated.

Joanna Penn, ALLi's enterprise and technology advisor, says:

1. Read the terms and conditions of the tools to ensure you have commercial usage of any output. You will usually need a paid subscription for this, depending on the tool.
2. Don't use artist or brand names in prompts as you might, even inadvertently, infringe someone else's copyright. For instance, don't ask for images in "the style of Pixar."
3. Use tutorials to discover how to make consistent characters across your images. This is available in some tools and will improve over time.
4. Be aware that the skills of an illustrator go way beyond "generating images," just as the skills of a writer go way beyond "generating words." Images are about meaning and connection and that takes skill and experience. A human illustrator can help match images to your words and will have the language to find the right images. Consider working with an illustrator who embraces AI tools, and you can make the most of the collaboration.

IMPORTANT LEGAL CONSIDERATIONS

Whatever images you use, whether in the book interior or on the cover, however they are generated, you must ensure you have the legal right to use them and that you understand if there are any restrictions.

Be sure you know who owns the rights to the cover design and how the cover can be used by both parties. If the designer has used stock pictures, there might be restrictions on the number of copies that may be printed, so ask about this.

If you hire an illustrator, check whether you keep the rights to the illustrations. Some illustrators will agree to this as a work-for-hire arrangement, some will not. It's very much a matter of personal choice.

FURTHER READING

ALLi Self-Publishing Services Directory Selfpublishingadvice.org/directory

Choose The Best Self-Publishing Services Selfpublishingadvice.org/ChooseBestServices

You can purchase your copies of these guides from Selfpublishingadvice.org/bookshop/ or if you're an ALLi member, get free access to the ebook versions in the members' zone. Just login and navigate to PUBLICATIONS.

6

PRINTING AND DISTRIBUTION

You need to print the book. You need to get it to customers, which involves distribution, storage and delivery. All of this might appear to be a daunting task, but there are many tools available to help self-publishing authors, and you may be pleasantly surprised by how simple the process can be.

PRINT PRODUCTION

Print on demand (POD)

POD was a revolution for indie authors. Previously we had to buy print runs and then store the copies, or pay for warehousing. Now, we can upload a PDF of the book to a printer, who prints a copy each time a customer orders one.

The front-runners for POD production are Amazon's Kindle Direct Publishing (KDP), Bookvault and IngramSpark. At the time of writing, IngramSpark and Bookvault provide a variety of trim sizes including the square (8x8 inches) size that is more common for picture books aimed at younger readers.

You can also use these printers for short runs of your book to take to school visits, book signings and other events, and to supply local bookshops directly. Each site has calculators to allow you to view author copy costs.

However, POD isn't suitable for all kinds of books. The unit costs can be high, especially for full-color interiors. The print quality may not be as good as a print run, which again is an issue for full-color books. And the choice of paper stock and trim sizes might be limited, and so your book might not look as beautifully finished next to a book from a large publisher. POD is great for books with limited interior artwork, but authors of children's picture books often use other print options.

Offset and speciality printing

Historically, offset printing has been the preferred method for large publishers because of economies of scale. Typically they will order several thousand copies in one go. This might not be cost-effective for indie authors unless you have a bestseller.

However, some children's authors use offset printing, most notably for color picture books. They might use Kickstarter and other crowdfunding methods to raise the upfront costs for a print run of 2,000 or more books. This strategy has a huge learning curve and requires heavy promotion, but it works for some authors.

Short digital print runs

One option that can successfully complement POD is short digital print runs in the low hundreds from independent printers who are not also acting as publishers (as Amazon KDP, IngramSpark and Bookvault are). Typically, you might do this to order stock for school or other events where you expect to sell in solid numbers. The unit costs will be lower than KDP Print, Bookvault, or IngramSpark author copies if you're ordering over 100 copies, and certainly if going toward 200. This will make sense if your cashflow allows for it, and you are certain there is demand.

In the case of picture books, short digital print runs also offer the chance to get silk-finish (coated) paper for your interior pages, something that is not offered by most POD companies at the time of writing. Again, ensure there is sufficient demand for your book as the upfront cost for interior color and coated paper is high.

Also keep in mind that if you're not in a country where the POD company has a print facility, you might experience longer wait times, higher shipping costs and taxes. This is particularly important if you need to stock books for visits to fairs or schools.

If you've worked with a professional illustrator and cover designer, they can help you with decisions about printers and special paper stock. They can also help you decide if proof copies are the right quality—two more reasons why these professionals are worth the investment. For more about print options, see this blog post from ALLi Partner Member MCRL Overseas Group: Selfpublishingadvice.org/your-questions-answered-illustrated-childrens-books/

PRINT BOOK DISTRIBUTION

Distribution is the process and logistics of getting your book to the consumer. Although distributing to online sellers is fairly simple, distributing to physical bookstores is more challenging.

It takes time to build up your authorial presence and sales, so unless you have a blockbuster debut, finding retailers to carry your book in store can be a significant challenge.

Second, there's the matter of wholesale discounting. There are several middle men between you and a physical bookstore—distributors take a cut, and the bookstore needs to make a profit too. Because of this, you need to set a wholesale discount on your cover price that gives everyone a little profit. Typically this is 55 percent. This is the industry standard for brick-and-mortar sales, and it will impact on your profits.

That said, it's definitely possible to get your books into bookstores.

If your books are set up on the Ingramspark or Bookvault POD services, bookshops will be able to order them. However, you'll need to approach stores individually and persuade them to stock you.

We've already discussed the importance of the wholesale discount. Another vital detail is to state whether you will accept returns. ALLi's advice is to choose "no" for returns. What does this mean? Most bookshops like to take books on a sale-or-return basis in case they don't sell. If they order these copies from your POD provider, the books will have been printed specially. So if they're then returned, someone has to pay for the printing—and that's you. So specify that you won't accept returns. However, this doesn't prevent the shop ordering your book if a customer asks for it, and this will be the most common scenario for your high-street book sales unless you hit the bestseller lists.

Also, you can supply the store yourself on a sale-or-return basis if you take the stock in personally. For some authors, this works very well. ALLi's Children's Publishing Advisor Karen Inglis has plenty of advice on how to approach local bookshops, working collaboratively with them on in-store events and school visits, and supporting them creatively through local PR and marketing. She also talks about pricing and setting wholesale discounts with IngramSpark for wider distribution, and why allowing returns is not generally a good idea except in rare circumstances. Find out more in *How to Self-Publish and Market a Children's Book*.

Selling direct from your website

For these reasons, indie authors tend not to focus so much on physical bookstore sales. But physical bookstores aren't the only game in town. Some of the POD services have plugins that make it easy to sell print books on your own website, and you can also customize books and send add-ons.

This blog post gives more detail on selling print books direct: Selfpublishingadvice.org/print-books-direct/

EBOOKS AND AUDIOBOOKS

While print books are undoubtedly attractive, your book can also be an ebook and an audiobook. In these formats, it's easy to reach readers all around the world through multiple retailers and libraries.

While picture books might be less friendly on an e-reader, books that are predominantly text work well. Not only are digital books cheaper for reader and author, they are easier to find in online stores. And they meet readers on the format they are already used to: their screen of choice. Most indie authors find that ebooks are the most lucrative format.

Audiobooks are becoming more popular too. Children are now as used to conversing with Alexa, Siri or another digital voice as they are with their friends. However, the cost of producing an audiobook can be daunting, so make sure you do your return-on-investment calculations.

DISTRIBUTING TO LIBRARIES

Indie authors can get their books into libraries through platforms like PublishDrive and Draft2Digital, which list on the databases that go to librarians. Many libraries work with multiple vendor partners, and ALLi advises that you list your book in as many outlets as possible. If you have time to do only one, Kobo Writing Life's arrangement with OverDrive gives wide access and the highest rates for a single-second click of a button.

Each library operates its own policy, ordering stock from catalogues or by its chosen book supplier. You can also approach libraries directly. To do this, check their websites for the head of the children's department or youth services. The library might publish a collection development policy that indicates the kinds of books it collects and whether it buys books or has them donated.

Whatever the methods of curation, libraries will be more prepared to take a risk on self-published titles over commercial because the pricing tends to be lower. But your book must look professional, credible and well-suited for the the library's community.

In short, libraries can be long term partners for your author business. You can find out more in ALLi's short guide, *Your Book in Libraries Worldwide*. This guidebook is free for members, and available to purchase for non-members at Selfpublishingadvice.org/BookInLibraries.

FURTHER READING

Your Book in Bookstores: ALLi's Guide to Print Book Distribution for Authors by Debbie Young is free for members, and available to purchase for non-members at Selfpublishingadvice.org/BookInBookstores.

How to Self-Publish and Market a Children's Book by Karen Inglis, Well Said Press

7

BUILDING YOUR BRAND AND COMMUNITY

It's time to talk about your author platform. This is anything that helps readers understand who you are as an author, what your books are about and where to buy them.

An author platform can be composed of many different aspects, but for most self-publishing children's authors it begins with:

- Your website (which might be transactional, so readers can buy your books there and then).
- Your mailing list or online community.
- A tribe-building medium such as a blog, podcast or YouTube channel.
- Social media channels–such as Facebook, Instagram, X, Pinterest, TikTok.

There is plenty of free advice available on using these options, and a good tip when starting out is to follow accounts of authors like you to see what they are doing. You can then decide which platform(s) feel like the right fit for you and start gradually.

However, a website is required at the very minimum. It tells readers and book buyers—parents, teachers, librarians—who you are, where to find your books, what's new with you, and how to contact you. If you want to be taken seriously as a writer, you need a website.

While you might sell books from your website, don't think of it merely as a shop. It should also tell your story. People can learn a lot about you from your website, so take the opportunity to share as much as you can with a combination of evergreen content and news updates (text and images) that truly reflects your writing life and your voice. This is all part of building your author brand.

Children's books, as we've discussed before, are evocative; using images, strong character voices and words they make children think, feel and dream. You can think beyond the words on the page, just like Disney does with Disneyland. While a theme park might not be in your plans at the moment, your website is your land.

As explained in ALLi's campaign guidebook, *SelfPub3: Author Business*, indie authors are now becoming more independent by placing their website at the center of their author business. And your website, especially if you are a children's author, can do more than just showcase you or your books. It can be a place for children and parents or teachers to gain more from.

Children's books are unique, marketing wise, because you don't actually market to your target audience. You market to the adults in their lives. So you might aim to reach one or other of them, or both. How do you do that?

Many ALLi author members do this by building an author website that keeps readers coming back.

- Mahtab Narsimhan, who writes fantasy for a range of ages, uses a simple and clear website design to reach teachers: Mahtabnarsimhan.com/
- Fiona Lowry, who writes picture books for ages 3-5, has a colorful website for her young readers: Fionalowryauthor.com/
- Tuula Pere, who writes picture books, chapter books, poems and short stories for a range of ages in both Finnish and Swedish, has a fun website that includes all her books including lots of pictures: Books.wickwick.fi/

Providing information

The most important purpose of a website is to provide information. While your readers will arrive on your website for varied reasons, there are a few key points that you should consider showcasing.

- Jerome Tiller, who adapts classic stories for a middle-grade audience and illustrates them, shares free samples with readers to give them a taste of the books: Adaptedclassics.com/photo-gallery
- John Shay, who writes picture books, also has a few sample pages for readers to browse before purchasing: Pandademick.com

Building worlds

World-building is an important element in fiction and in some non-fiction. Some ALLi members are opening up their book-worlds on their websites, offering readers more about their characters, creating maps, rule guides for their settings and much more.

These guides are great for building their brand, and also for marketing the books to new readers giving them an appetiser before they embark on the journey.

- NM Rosen, who writes books that bring families together, has a comprehensive website that invites families to participate: Professorstork.com
- Jackie Loxham has a website for her middle-grade character that takes readers to settings in the books and gives the story behind each landmark. Ottillee-bottomly.com
- Rae Knightly, who writes teen science-fiction adventures, gives readers scientific facts and explains scientific concepts: Raeknightly.com
- Stuart White, who writes middle-grade sci-fi, steps back and lets his character introduces readers to the story: Stuartwhiteauthor.co.uk

- Jeffrey Lindberg, who writes picture books based on his long fascination with Coney Island in New York, provides the story behind the book and illustrations which are as captivating as the story itself: Coneybook.com/about-the-book
- Kathy Cherry writes adventure books set in a national park. On her website she shares a map of the real-life setting and her passion for helping out wildlife: Kathycherrybooks.com/do-something/
- Jess Lohmann, who writes middle-grade stories, has a "which character are you" quiz: Jesslohmann.com/quiz/
- Nicholas J Nawroth and Ellen Kennedy, who write the Papa Paws books for children up to the age of 5, has illustrations of his characters next to their real life inspiration. The website also offers youngsters coloring pages: Papaandpaws.com/characters/
- Stephen Haunts, who writes middle-grade sci-fi, shares a guide to Mars, which is like a rule-book for the story world: Stephenhauntsfiction.com/diary-of-a-martian

All these sites offer a rich bonus experience that attracts readers to the authors' work.

When devising bonus content, always keep in mind your overall brand. Ensure your website materials and your books have a consistent voice and feel.

Clubs and activities for kids

Whatever age group you are writing for, most children enjoy being part of a club and engaging in creative activities. Many indie authors use activities and clubs as platforms to engage their readers and also to create a conducive environment for families to do something creative together. You can customize activities to suit your author brand and books. Here are a few examples:

- Deb Cushman, who writes fantasy adventure books for

children and teens, has a clubhouse based in her fictional world for all members of the family: Debcushman.com
- DM Miller, who writes middle-grade novels in fantasy and contemporary settings, has a page of downloadable crosswords, puzzles and coloring exercises: Dmmiller.org/downloads/
- Ronesa Aveela, who writes mystery romance inspired by folklore, shares recipes that have cultural significance for her character: Ronesaaveela.wordpress.com/marias-kitchen/
- Cheryl Johnson, who writes books inspired by the natural world for children aged 3-10, has downloadable activity sheets and calendars: Cheryljohnsonauthor.com/childrens-books/activity-sheets/
- Alicia Carbo-Guha, who writes environmentally inspired books for children aged 6-8, offers coloring books for children: Aliciacarboguha.com/fun-stuff
- B Random, who writes middle-grade science fiction adventures, has writing prompts for readers to try out: B-random.space/?page_id=185
- Lexi Rees, who writes activity books and action-adventure books for a range of readers, offers creative writing courses for children: Lexirees.co.uk/creative-writing-courses-for-kids/
- Peta Rainford writes picture books on plastic pollution and offers awareness-raising tips for young readers: Dogpigeon.co.uk/?page_id=2457
- Dan Bailes writes books with animal characters and provides fun facts and extras on his website: Nicedogbooks.com/fun-extras/

Resources for adults

Never forget, the people actually purchasing your books are adults. So many authors offer website resources for this important audience.

- Amy Flanagan, who writes stories about a dog who is a lawyer, provides teachers a list of questions to discuss with

their students when studying her books: Mrsrsnugglesworth.com/teacher-resources
- Julie Anne Penn, who writes stories about common emotional challenges in the first years of school, provides parenting tips: Teamsupercrew.com/team-supercrew-blog
- Scott Peters, who writes middle-grade mysteries inspired by historical periods, provides activity sheets for teachers and students with an FAQ section: Scottpetersbooks.com/
- Kari Dunn Buron, who writes books for children with autism spectrum disorders, creates non-fiction resources for parents to help children express their emotions: 5pointscale.com/downloadables.html

FURTHER READING

ALLi's campaign guidebook *SelfPub3: Author Business* is free for members, and available to purchase for non-members at *Selfpublishingadvice.org/Book/SelfPub3*.

8

MEETING YOUNG READERS
SCHOOL AND LIBRARY VISITS

School and library visits, whether hosted in person or online, allow you to reach children where they are.

Most schools and libraries welcome visits from authors and have an annual budget for this. Libraries love hosting story hours with local authors, and most libraries have weekly scheduled story times, with lots of children and parents attending regularly. Larger libraries even offer multiple story times for different age groups, making the targeting of your book's audience even easier.

For authors, these events are a great opportunity to engage with readers and understand what they enjoy reading. For the book-buying adults, meeting you provides the rapport and confidence they need to make a purchase.

How do you find opportunities?

Get in touch with a local school administrator or librarian and build a relationship with them.

Here are some tips:

- Establish the connection. A good place to begin is your local library (that you frequent), the school you went to, or the school your young ones attend. When you make the first contact, let them know how you're connected to their organization.
- Think like them. Put yourself in the teacher or the librarian's perspective. What do they need? If you're in the US, a great place to start is the state standards for your target age range. In the UK, you can look at the key stages. Later you can use this information when building your presentation. And decide if you are going to do classroom or assembly presentations or both. The method of delivery matters especially when it's online.
- Do your research. Look at the school's website and make sure you're contacting the correct person and not the staff member tasked with managing the school's accounts. In schools, you could look for the head librarian, the reading resource teacher, the language teacher, or even the principal or head. When contacting a library, ask the reception or help desk who you should talk to.
- Create postcards, make calls, and write emails (or all three) focusing on the outcome for students and library users followed by testimonials from other schools. Testimonials build confidence in you and your work. These also help indicate if you are a good fit for their young audience.
- Be patient, but don't be afraid to send out reminders. Teachers and librarians have a full workload, but authors often find that despite weeks of silence, a reminder can do the trick and they are met with enthusiasm and kindness. So don't assume silence means "no." Be professional and ask again.

In the UK, some schools have a Patron of Reading scheme, where a specific author collaborates with teachers and children throughout the academic year. Patrons of Reading might host workshops, activities and recommend books for different reading levels. Sue Wickstead, who writes picture and coloring books for readers age 5-8, hosts craft workshops: Suewickstead.co.uk/school-visits/design-a-bus-workshop

If you pitch your book to the children's department at a library, it's worth also asking about staging an event. An event is a great way to get on your library's radar, meet the staff and local readers. Karen Inglis, ALLi's Children's Publishing Advisor, says: "I did a children's event at my local library, which was a good way to get exposure. I recently discovered that one of my books subsequently had 72 library borrows, thanks just to that visit."

Lynne Jorritsma, who writes rhyming picture books, says she was invited to a library after a bookstore event. "After an employee at the local library saw me at a bookstore event, they asked me to facilitate a children's reading time."

Planning and conducting a school or library visit

A school or library visit is not like a typical book reading, where the author reads to an audience.

Children don't have long attention spans. They need interaction, conversations and games to keep them interested.

As well as the content, there are practicalities to consider. Lois Hoffman, founder of The Happy Self-Publisher and the author of a children's picture book, says: "Provide the school with any technical requirements, discuss the timing of your performance or performances, inform the school if you need help to navigate the building, provide forms for ordering your books, and let the school know of any pre-event activities that would enhance the presentation or build excitement about the visit. Most importantly, practice your presentation (a lot) and also test your tech setup. Children are not likely to be patient with tech glitches or delays. On the day of the visit, wear comfortable shoes and be prepared for anything. Children are never predictable."

Whether you're at a school or a library, have fun with your visits. Get creative, involve the kids in your reading, let them ask questions, and bring silly props or costumes that relate to your book. And don't forget to bring print copies on the day to sign and sell. Lynne Jorritsma took printouts from her spot-the-difference coloring book for a coloring session.

You don't need to be perfect but use every library or school visit to learn about your readers, your books, and improve your presentation skills.

BOOK FAIRS

Many children's authors have had success at book fairs.

Lynne Jorritsma finds out about local book events from other author friends. "I'm part of a local author's group in the Netherlands, so we hear about fairs through that. These are often for the international community. I found out about others by doing a simple search on Google."

HOLDING INVENTORY

Whether you're selling at book fairs, schools, libraries or bookshop events, you'll need inventory. As discussed in Chapter 6 "Printing and Distribution", this is reasonably straightforward if you're in the countries that POD services like IngramSpark, Bookvault, or KDP print in. Otherwise, your costs can be higher especially if your print sizes are not very common.

Lynne Jorristma, in the Netherlands, says she could order a bulk run with a printer there, but she finds POD cheaper even though there is added tax post Brexit.

WHY IT'S WORTH DOING FACE-TO-FACE EVENTS

While face-to-face events might seem like a waste of precious writing time, especially with the preparation, travel and printing costs, they give you an excellent opportunity to talk to potential customers and hear what they like. You'll also meet other authors like you and build your network.

It's vital to be professional, says Lynne Jorristma, in your approach, the look and quality of your books, and the delivery of your presentations. "If you're professional, the attitude to indie authors is positive in the Netherlands. We have met some great supporters who really want to see indies succeed."

FURTHER READING

For more tips on reaching out to libraries, bookshops and schools, see the "Ultimate Guide to Selling Children's Books" which includes case studies from two very different authors Selfpublishingadvice.org/the-ultimate-guide-to-selling-childrens-books/

Also see the ALLi guide *Your Book In Libraries*. You can purchase a copy at Selfpublishingadvice.org/BookInLibraries or, as an ALLi member, download the ebook free in the members' zone.

9

MARKETING A CHILDREN'S BOOK ONLINE

Real-life visits are great for marketing, but they're not the whole story. Don't neglect digital promotion.
What you do will vary according to the kind of books you write—the genre and age and niche that you're targeting.

ALLi's Children's Publishing Advisor Karen Inglis gives these tips in *How to Market a Children's Book*.

10-STEP CHILDREN'S BOOK MARKETING PLAN

1. Include marketing links and messages (including email sign-up incentives) in your book's back matter.
2. Complete your Amazon author bio page in all the key markets—take a look at competitor authors' pages for ideas.
3. Create an online presence with a website or blog and include a mailing list sign-up there too.
4. Add social media if you use them.
5. Approach local libraries, bookshops, schools, playgroups and any relevant visitor centers.
6. Contact local press, magazines, community websites.
7. Research local events and fairs.

8. Provide a free copy of your book to your beta readers and ask for an honest review.
9. Research and approach children's book review sites, bloggers, individual reviewers, and research children's books giveaway programs.
10. Experiment with Amazon advertising and research other advertising options.

Steps 1 and 2 are crucial and should be in place before you start marketing.

You'll find a lot more detail on these steps in Karen's book.

Should you outsource your marketing?

Hiring a service to help you market and promote your book—and you—is tricky. Some will give good value, as they will have contacts that are exactly right for your book and that you wouldn't be able to find for yourself. But bear in mind that there is no other service where you are more vulnerable to having your dreams of success exploited. Only outsource your marketing if the service will add real value and if you have budget to spare. You know your book the best, and you are its best sales person.

Do your due diligence on the service before you hire them. ALLi's *Self-Publishing Services Directory* can help you. See Chapter 12: "Resources".

REVIEWS

Reviews are the holy grail for children's authors and are harder to come by than for books for adults or the YA market. That's because your readers are not buying directly, and some may be too young to post online. Also, because most children's books are read in print rather than digital formats, it is less easy to entice a reader to click a link and post a spur-of-the-moment review when they get to the last page.

But there are ethical tactics that children's authors can use to get reviews. They include:

- Connecting with local schools and libraries when your book first comes out and offering free copies as part of your launch, with a request for an honest review online in return, but without obligation.
- Requesting reviews at the back of your book alongside other marketing messages such as links to free downloads of posters, puzzles or other material relating to the book. Note that any sign-ups for email newsletters must be done by an adult and this should be clearly stated.
- Connecting with bloggers who specialize in children's book reviews.
- Using online platforms such as BookSirens or StoryOrigin to connect with children's book reviewers.

For more details, including the data protection rules for newsletter signups, see Karen Inglis's book.

Paid Review Services

The reviews we've discussed so far are from customers and bloggers. These are usually given free, although you may pay a small fee to be listed on a database.

It is also possible to pay for reviews from industry experts. These are known as editorial reviews. They are intended to be professional, unbiased, critical evaluations and will be posted on the organization's website, where other influential people will see them. These reviews might have a long reach. For example, at the time of writing, BlueInk Review states that its reviews are posted not only on its website and newsletter, but also syndicated to the Children's Literature Comprehensive Database and posted on Ingram's database and Goodreads. Blueink also places reviews of selected self-published titles in *Booklist* magazine, which is read by 60,000 librarians.

Editorial reviews can bring you much-needed critical heft, but bear in mind that the review may not be positive. While most services give you the option to suppress a negative review, there are no refunds if the reviewer posts a scathing assessment of your work.

AWARDS AND CONTESTS

Winning a book award can be a catalyst for discovery, raising you out of obscurity and into the spotlight. The value of that spotlight might vary greatly, but recognition from an esteemed panel of judges can increase a book's credibility, visibility and marketability.

A few contests offer cash prizes to top winners, and the best awards give you usable feedback even if you don't win the main award. And a win or a placing is a good marketing tool for you. You can display medals and stickers on your book, website and email signature, and include them in pitch letters to schools, libraries and other event organizers. But there are now a lot of awards on offer to indie authors and some members report that winning has made little difference to book sales, no matter how hard they market their award.

Also, contests can be expensive, especially if you are entering a number of them. Entry fees are usually between $75 and $200 USD per category. As well as the entry fee, there's the cost of shipping multiple copies of your printed book, sometimes overseas, though ebooks can generally be uploaded for free.

So, as with all paid services, beware. Some book awards are set up to make money for the organizers rather than recognize the accomplishments of the entrants. And it's a murky area because the costs of running a contest can be high. Also, there are very few non-profit contests. Most contests produce good revenue for the organizers and sponsors, in financial terms and also in increased traffic to their website as you spread the news of your progress on social media.

So enter any book award contest only after careful consideration and review of its reputation. Compare fees and read about possible additional expenses if you win, such as purchasing stickers for your book, contributing to publicity costs or attending award ceremonies. Check their reputations on ALLi's Watchdog Desk and our Awards and Contests Ratings page, which includes children's book awards. You'll find it at Selfpublishingadvice.org/awards

MARKETING THROUGH DISCOUNTS AND PERMANENTLY FREE EBOOKS

Offering the first ebook in a series for free, or at a heavily discounted price, is a common long-term marketing strategy used by authors of books for adults and young adults.

For children's authors, this strategy could make sense if you write in a series at the older end of the middle-grade age group. Readers who enjoy your free or 99p/99c book might go on to buy the other books in the series at full price. Parents may also buy or download the free or discounted ebook to check the content before buying in print for a child. This long-term "loss leader" strategy can be very effective.

However, this tactic can also be a slippery slope. Some authors resort to lowering the price of all of their ebooks to compete in an intensely crowded field. This sets a precedent of devaluing books that some experts feel can be harmful in the long run. Readers who grow accustomed to free and heavily discounted books may eschew regularly priced books, which is not good for author income. For this reason, we don't recommend lowering the price of all of your ebooks. Value your books appropriately, and reserve discounts for special promotions and incentives.

BOOK PROMOTION

While marketing and promotion might sound like synonyms, they are not. Marketing is long term and ongoing. It's the process by which you constantly try to raise awareness of your books and find new readers. Promotions are different. They are short-term campaigns, limited-time incentives to attract interest.

Promotions might be limited-time markdowns, free-download days, giveaways, contests and other events to boost your revenue and bring in new readers. Those readers may go on to buy other titles now or in the future and might even become lifelong fans.

PRESS RELEASES

Press releases are a staple of traditional marketing and an important means of connecting with the mainstream media. But indie authors now have many other ways of finding readers, many of them more effective than a press release. For some authors, press releases produce a good result. For others, they don't. Like everything, it's only by exploring and experimenting that you can know whether press releases are worthwhile for your particular books.

The quality of the contacts is paramount when sending out press releases. For children's books, we recommend keeping your PR efforts local because you're more likely to strike a chord. Write the release yourself (instead of hiring a publicist), and send it to local websites, news outlets, newsletters and magazines. Sending your releases further afield is unlikely to result in coverage unless you have an exceptional news hook.

An effective press release is one that is carefully tailored to the recipients and carefully targeted to those most likely to broadcast news of the book. You need to write to them as though you already understand what they need—as you did when approaching schools and librarians.

There are companies that offer press release services that essentially blast a press release to a massive mailing list that is probably not suitable for your book, and possibly also out of date. Also avoid services that simply post your press release on a website. A shotgun approach will not work here.

Beware also of publishing services that charge a hefty markup for creating a press release. This is often the hallmark of vanity press.

FURTHER READING

ALLi's guidebook *Reach More Readers, Sell More Books: ALLi's Guide to Book Marketing for Authors and Poets* will help you create a marketing plan for your books. Buy a copy at Selfpublishingadvice.org/MarketingBook or, as an ALLi member, download the ebook free in the members' zone.

How to Market a Children's Book by Karen Inglis. Well Said Press

10

ONE BOOK, MANY FORMATS

At the time of writing, ALLi's Children's Publishing Advisor Karen Inglis has sold rights to 12 countries for her international bestselling middle-grade time-travel adventure *The Secret Lake*. China and the Czech Republic have also bought the rights to the sequel *Return to the Secret Lake*.

These deals all came from unsolicited approaches from overseas publishers who saw *The Secret Lake*'s success in the US, Canada and the UK. And they show the potential of licensing rights.

WHAT IS RIGHTS LICENSING?

A book is more than an ebook, print book or audiobook; it is a suite of publishing rights that you can exploit—for translations, merchandise, TV versions and other adaptations. You can either make these versions yourself if that's feasible, or you can trade and license them. However, when trading and licensing your rights, be aware of giving away too much—this is known as the rights grab.

Here's a cautionary tale. A children's book author who was an ALLi member crafted a charming character that was adapted into a BBC children's TV program. The show achieved significant success, and spawned a line of merchandise that continues to delight young audiences several years on. Happy days? Alas not. The author unwittingly signed away all her subrights (and also agreed to other constrictive clauses about reversion and length of copyright).

As the author's creation found new life and popularity on screen and in merchandise, she did not receive any royalties or recognition from these lucrative extensions. Not one penny. And despite our best efforts and legal advice, the situation remains unchanged. She does not have the resources to go into a full legal campaign.

This is the most extreme example we have seen at ALLi, but it shows you need to protect yourself when negotiating a rights contract. Follow these guiding principles:

1. Understand the contract. Be clear on what you are signing away and what you're gaining. Most of us don't understand legal jargon, and it is within your right to ask questions until you understand.
2. Selectively license your rights. Don't sign away all your rights. Make sure the other party has the ability to optimally exploit the rights you are licensing to them. For instance, a TV company doesn't need your translation rights, for example. And a publisher translating into French doesn't need your German rights too.
3. Limit the territory. Be as protective as possible with the territories you are signing rights away to. Make sure it is in your best business interest to do so.
4. Limit the term. A term of 3 to 5 years is enough for a publisher to exploit the rights it is licensing from you. You can always renew the contract after this term. Be wary of contracts that demand you sign away long periods of time or the lifetime of copyright.
5. Don't fear the negotiation. Publishers are your business partners, and like any business agreement, they are open to negotiating. Learn the art of negotiation and put your best foot forward.

You don't have to wait for offers to come to you. You can seek deals yourself. Or you might hire your own translators, merchandising companies and partners for specific territories. For most indie authors, it's a cost-benefit analysis depending on the market size for their books.

ALLi's guidebook *How Authors Sell Publishing Rights* gives details about rights contracts, finding opportunities, and negotiations. This guidebook is free for members, and available to purchase for non-members at Selfpublishingadvice.org/rightsbook

FINDING YOUR OWN TRANSLATOR

You can find translators in the ALLi *Self-Publishing Services Directory*, which has vetted, approved and experienced translators. This directory is free for members, and available to purchase for non-members at Selfpublishingadvice.org/directory. Another good source is Reedsy.

Quality translation isn't cheap. We recommend venturing into translation only if your book is selling well enough to afford a translator, which could cost several thousand dollars, depending on the length of the book. And before you do that, there are other, better investments you can make before translation, like audiobooks.

Or if your language skills are good enough, you might translate the books yourself, as ALLi member Skye Mackinnon does, with the picture books she writes as Isla Wynter: Islawynter.com/index.html

Here's another angle that children's book writers can exploit—early childhood educator Sarah McPherson has created separate versions of her books for boys and girls: Sarahmcphersonauthor.com.au/books-books-books/

MERCHANDISING

Merchandising rights can be sold separately but they are, more times than not, packaged along with other larger, lucrative rights like TV or serial rights.

This is something authors can also do themselves. There are POD services to create mugs, T-shirts and other items, and many authors are selling these to readers via their own website. If you're putting your illustrations or covers on merchandise, make sure you have the legal rights to the artwork and don't have to buy a separate license.

- Mother-daughter team Terrel and Konora write the Once Upon A Dance books about dancing. They sell posters, mugs, pillows, cards and other swag: Onceuponadance.com
- Alessa Ellefson illustrated her own books and has created merchandise from the artwork: Alessaellefson.com
- Rebecca Victor has created stickers and magnets from her picture books and some more unusual items that help children play in the story world, such as flight goggles and a plush toy: 085f40.myshopify.com
- Merchandise can appeal to older age groups too. Elizabeth Stevens has created special college T-shirts and phone cases for her YA readers: Elizabethstevens.com.au/merchandise-1
- And how about a fully customizable book with the child's name and appearance? Artist Leo Hartas and writer Amanda Boulter have used POD to create Wow That's Me books Wowthatsme.com/

FURTHER READING

ALLi's guidebook *How Authors Sell Publishing Rights* is free for members, and available to purchase for non-members at Selfpublishingadvice.org/rightsbook

PART III
RESOURCES AND SUPPORT

Resources, FAQs and other links to help you in your journey as a children's author.

11

FREQUENTLY ASKED QUESTIONS

How long does it take to publish a children's book?

Give yourself at least a year from concept to completion. Much depends on the length of the book—a YA novel will clearly take longer than a picture book with far fewer words.

That said, if you're working with an illustrator, good illustrations take time. There might also be a waiting period before your chosen illustrator can get to your project.

And the publishing process doesn't end with the creation. Good editing takes time, as does proper formatting. You also need to give proper time to setting up the marketing and promotion.

With all that in mind, a year isn't an unreasonable timescale. Bear in mind, though, that much of that is learning the ropes and you'll get faster with subsequent books.

How much does it cost to publish a children's book?

Children's books are generally shorter than books for adults, but that doesn't mean they're cheaper to produce.

Illustrations for children's picture books can cost anywhere between $2,000 and $10,000, though they generally don't exceed $6,000.

Your book needs cover artwork. If the interior artwork isn't suitable or you don't have interior artwork, you'll need a cover designer, which can cost between $200 and $700.

Your experience as a publisher will affect the costs: a more polished manuscript, for example, will be less expensive to edit. If your book is predominantly text, the interior will be less costly to format, though the costs of this also vary with the book's length. For that reason, we're a little wary of giving estimates when individual cases differ so much.

That said, if we absolutely have to give a ballpark figure for the cost of self-publishing a children's book, we'd say you should expect to spend at least $5,000.

12

RESOURCES

WHERE CAN I GET HELP AND ADVICE?

- We recommend the SCBWI, the children's book author association which has more than 70 regional chapters around the world and allows you to network with local, likeminded children's authors: SCBWI.com. SCBWI has an official blog for and by authors: Scbwi.blogspot.com/ and its useful list of awards and grants Scbwi.org/awards-and-grants
- We also recommend the Children's Literature Association (ChLA), which takes a more academic approach to children's books and can give you great insights: Childlitassn.org.
- You can find countless other literary organizations and creative forums online. Joining a community of children's authors helps you learn about the world of children's literature while making writer friends and developing a professional support system.
- *How to Self-publish and Market a Children's Book* by Karen Inglis. Well Said Press.
- Karen's blog for children's book authors: SelfPublishingAdventures.com
- This blog by former literary agent Mary Kole: Kidlit.com/

- The Purple Crayon, a blog by children's book editor Harold Underdown: Underdown.org/
- The Children's Book Insider, a paid membership site offering plenty of worthwhile advice on all aspects of the genre: Cbiclubhouse.com/clubhouse/kb/
- The Adventures in YA Publishing blog, which provides advice, workshops, giveaways and more: Adventuresinyapublishing.com/

ALLi Publications and Other Resources

- ALLi's guide to basic self-publishing questions *150 Self-Publishing Questions Answered: ALLi's Writing, Publishing, & Book Marketing Tips for Authors and Poets*: Selfpublishingadvice.org/150SelfPublishingQuestions
- ALLi's other self-publishing guidebooks, some of which are mentioned in earlier chapters.
- ALLi's *Self-Publishing Services Directory* Selfpublishingadvice.org/directory/ to find our approved Partner Members.

Members can download ALLi publishing guides for free in the members' zone at: Allianceindependentauthors.org/publishing-guidebooks/. Non-members can browse and buy them at: Selfpublishingadvice.org/ShopCompleteGuides

- ALLi's blogpost on children's publishing: Selfpublishingadvice.org/successfully-self-publishing-childrens-books-alli-guide/
- ALLi's blog for more general self-publishing advice: SelfPublishingAdvice.org/blog
- ALLi's service ratings as researched by ALLi's Watchdog Desk: Selfpublishingadvice.org/ratings
- ALLi's weekly Self-publishing Advice Podcasts for inspiration and advice, with director Orna Ross and members of the ALLi

expert team: Allianceindependentauthors.org/askalli-podcast/
- The ALLi blog for the latest self-publishing news: Selfpublishingadvice.org/news
- ALLi's annual conference SelfPublishingAdvice Conference.com: The largest online gathering of independent authors, each October
- Guidance for your creative and business planning: Go! Creative planning program run by Orna Ross: Patreon.com/OrnaRoss

ACKNOWLEDGMENTS

All good books are a team effort. An author's name goes on the cover but behind that is the creative team of editors and designers and formatters who made the book, the distributors and marketers who take it to readers, and the long list of supporters—from family members to work colleagues—without whom it would never have been created.

Then there are the other writers, from journalists and academics to storytellers and poets, who have published ideas, information, and inspirations that, quite literally, underwrite the book.

All this is true for this book that you hold in your hand, and our thanks go to all those who had a hand in its making.

Thanks are due to all at the Alliance of Independent Authors (ALLi). ALLi guides rely heavily on the work and wisdom of our team, members, ambassadors and advisors. All of this is generously and freely shared with our non-profit CIC (Community Interest Company), with the intention of paying it forward and benefitting other indie authors. Thank you for your generosity and for lighting the way.

For this guide, particular thanks are due to ALLi's Children's Publishing Advisor Karen Inglis. We are indebted to her experience and wisdom. Thank you also to ALLi Members Lynne Jorritsma and Lois Hoffman for their advice and contribution.

Also Laurie Millie at SCWBI, ALLi director Orna Ross, Publications Manager Shanaya Wagh, publishing assistant Sarah Begley, cover designer Jane Dixon-Smith, ALLi Content and Communications strategist Sacha Black, and editors Roz Morris and Lauren Johnson. And to Literature and Latté, and the two Brads for creating Scrivener and Vellum software.

We are a small team behind ALLi, and we use technology to support our writing and publishing, including tools powered by AI (artificial and augmented intelligence). For this guidebook, we used Google's search engine, Word, Vellum, Zoom, ProWriting Aid, online dictionaries and thesaurus, as well as picking ChatGPT's brain, and interrogating various angles to ensure we'd thought through all the facets of self-publishing children's and YA books. Many of these tools are powered by AI. This does not mean this guidebook wasn't crafted by human creatives. ALLi books are, and always will be, crafted by authors for authors.

For this book and all our work together: thank you all.

OTHER GUIDES

Browse and buy more publishing guides for indie authors on our website: SelfPublishingAdvice.org/Bookshop

ABOUT ALLI

The Alliance of Independent Authors (ALLi) is the only global, non-profit association for self-publishing writers. ALLi aims to foster excellence and ethics in self-publishing; to support authors in the making and selling of their books; and to advocate for author independence through the building of sustainable digital businesses.

ALLi is pronounced "ally" (al-eye not al-ee), and we aim to be an ally to self-publishers everywhere. We unite thousands of beginner, emerging, and experienced indie authors from all over the world behind this mission. Most of our members are in the US and Canada, followed closely by Europe, Australia and New Zealand, and South Africa. We are a Community Interest Company (CIC) and all profits are invested back in for the benefit of our members and the wider indie author community.

Our work is fourfold:

- ALLi *advises*, providing best-practice information and education through our online Self-Publishing Advice Center, SelfPublishingAdvice.org, offering a daily blog, a weekly live video and podcast, a bookstore of self-publishing guidebooks, and a quarterly member magazine.
- ALLi *monitors* the self-publishing sector through a watchdog desk, alerting authors to bad actors and predatory players and running an approved partner program.
- ALLi *campaigns* for the advancement of indie authors in the publishing and literary sectors globally (bookstores, libraries, literary events, prizes, grants, awards, and other author organizations), encouraging the provision of publishing and business skills for authors, speaking out against iniquities and

inequities, and furthering the indie author cause wherever possible.
- ALLi *empowers* independent authors through community and collaboration—author forums, contract advice, sample agreements, contacts and networking, literary agency representation, and a member care desk.

Learn more about the Alliance of Independent Authors on our member website found at Allianceindependentauthors.org and the Self-Publishing Advice Center which is available for all indie authors at Selfpublishingadvice.org/about.

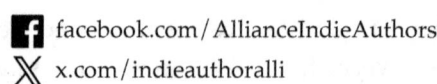

facebook.com/AllianceIndieAuthors
x.com/indieauthoralli

www.ingramcontent.com/pod-product-compliance
Lightning Source LLC
Chambersburg PA
CBHW072104110526
44590CB00018B/3304